FISH!
STICKS™

Also available:

FISH!: A Remarkable Way to Boost Morale and Improve Results
FISH! TALES: Real-Life Stories to Help You Transform Your
Workplace and Your Life

A Remarkable Way to Adapt to Changing
Times and Keep Your Work Fresh

FISH! STICKS™

Stephen C. Lundin, Ph.D.,
John Christensen, and Harry Paul

HYPERION

New York

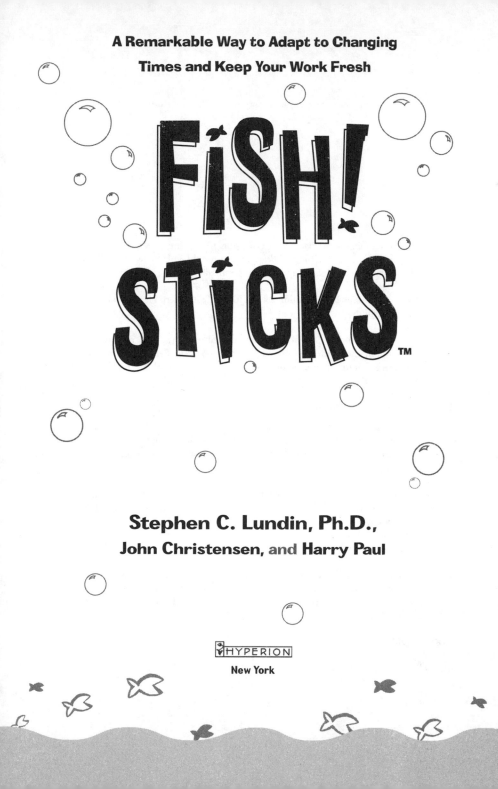

Grateful acknowledgment is made for permission to reprint copyrighted material from "The Journey" from *The House of Belonging*, copyright © 1997 by David Whyte, published by Many Rivers Press. Reprinted by permission of the publisher.

Library of Congress Cataloging-in-Publication Data

Lundin, Stephen C.
    Fish! sticks : a remarkable way to adapt to changing times and keep your work fresh / Stephen C. Lundin, Harry Paul, and John Christensen.—1st ed.
      p. cm.
    ISBN 0-7868-6816-3
    1. Organizational change.   2. Organizational behavior.   I. Title: Remarkable way to adapt to changing times and keep your work fresh.   II. Paul, Harry, 1950–   III. Christensen, John, 1959–   IV. Title.
    HD58.8 .L86   2003
    658.4'063—dc21   2002038708

Hyperion books are available for special quantity discounts to use as premiums or for special programs, including corporate training. For details contact Hyperion Special Markets, 77 West 66th Street, 11th floor, New York, New York 10023, or call 212-456-0133.

FIRST EDITION

10 9 8 7 6 5 4 3 2 1

INTRODUCTION

Some say change is difficult. I say change is a piece of cake (or perhaps cheese). If you want a real challenge, try to *sustain* a change—especially a change that requires commitment from all who do the work.

It doesn't matter if you are an individual contributor who wants to hang on to a better work life or a CEO who wants to maintain a new high level of productivity: Sustaining change is the true test of leadership. Holding on to a culture of innovation, maintaining a higher quality of work life, constantly renewing an important customer service program, or retaining a more participative management style requires the use of a unique set of principles that are different from those used simply to initiate a change.

A large-scale change usually comes with a lot of fanfare, so in the beginning there is considerable energy. It's typical to have meetings, training programs, off-sites, balloons, buttons, contests, pocket cards, newsletter articles, posters, and videos. And there is absolutely nothing wrong with any of these. External energy is often what it takes to catch our attention in a busy world. But external energy cannot sustain a change. That takes a different source of energy: natural energy.

When the balloons have deflated, the contests have ended, the training is complete, and the natural human tendency to look for the next new thing has started to exert itself, that is when the inevitable gravity pull of old ways sets in. When you are part of such an effort it feels like someone just took her foot off of the accelerator.

This gravity pull takes many forms, including distraction, busyness, resistance, boredom, forgetfulness, cynicism, and sabotage, to name a few. It doesn't really matter what is at stake—a new diet or a new way to be at work—all worthwhile changes are susceptible to the forces of gravity. Successful efforts to counteract these forces in order to sustain change is what separates the great workplaces and great people from the pack.

After teaching change management to MBA and corporate seminar students for twenty years and operating my own business in an environment where change was a constant, I coauthored the book *FISH!* and worked on a film of the same name. Ever since, I have had the privilege of observing organizations using the ideas in *FISH!* (as well as principles from other management books) to address a variety of important issues and to create positive change. The most pressing workplace needs addressed by those who turn to the FISH! Philosophy include improving the quality of work life, customer service, employee retention, the facility for innovation, productivity, and recruitment. Another reason people turn to it is simply to learn how to have more fun at work.

Over the last three years I have traveled almost a million miles speaking to and visiting with those who, in one way or another, are working to implement important organizational changes. I have been especially inspired by change efforts that were sustained after the excitement of the initial rollout had waned. There is a bounty of energy present when something is new—but a year later it takes a deeper source of energy to keep it going. I have seen many successful organizations that have found that source. Any wisdom demonstrated by the characters in this book has been extracted from real people sustaining change in real organizations. The World Famous Pike

Place Fish market, the inspiration for *FISH!*, is of course one of the many ongoing success stories from which we have learned valuable lessons.

This book is the work of my imagination, but it is based on many experiences the three of us have had over the last few years. John Christensen continues to make FISH! the main focus of his company, ChartHouse International, a place where stories are routinely collected in the course of business and where the language of possibilities rules. Harry Paul has found a life on the road speaking and consulting about FISH! It is a rare day that Harry doesn't have something to share.

Yes, we now stand on the shoulders of thousands who have brought new possibilities into their workplaces and their lives. Some have failed, some have succeeded, and for many it is too early to tell. But we have learned from them all. *FISH! STICKS* is designed to highlight the special set of commitments involved in keeping *any* worthwhile change alive. It is truly your story: I just happened to write it.

Stephen C. Lundin
Lutsen, Minnesota, USA
Fall 2002

FISH! STICKS ™

External energy is necessary at the beginning of any large-scale change initiative. To implement a new vision, you must first have everyone's attention.

But external energy is only effective for the short term. Eventually, external energy must be replaced by natural energy in order for the change to stick.

Brunch at Brunch

Rhonda and Will Bullock have a Sunday routine. Rhonda sings in a gospel choir and Will sits in the first pew with the kids. Then it's off to the nursing home to spend some time with Grandma. On special Sundays, like today, the next stop is the mall, where the kids chow down on fast food while Rhonda and Will look on in amazement during the ninety seconds it takes the kids to make the food disappear. Then Will walks the kids and the baby-sitter to the cinema while Rhonda waits in line for a booth at a wonderful little restaurant called, appropriately, *Brunch*.

This Sunday as Rhonda waited in line for Will to return, her mind drifted to the Good Samaritan Hospital, cornerstone of the Good Samaritan Hospital System of two dozen hospitals and clinics throughout New Jersey and the whole tristate region. Good Samaritan had been her employer for eleven years, and as she thought about work she could feel herself growing tense.

"Hey. Do I detect a frown instead of the usual smile?"

"You caught me thinking about Good Samaritan, Will. Sorry. I'm guilty of violating our number one rule for Sunday: no work. . . . Did you have any trouble finding a movie suitable for an eleven-year-old boy who thinks he is an adult and a seven-year-old girl who brings her doll to the theater?"

"The usual. Mike tried to convince me that *Return of Shaft* would be a good movie to see even though it is R rated. He said Shaft could be a great role model, and he promised he would hold his hands over his sister's eyes during the bad parts. Mia was willing to go wherever her big brother suggested, of course, but I explained that they needed to find a G or PG movie. They settled on the new Harry Potter film. Ann said it was great."

For a brief moment Rhonda saw the shining face of her wonderful stepdaughter, Ann, now twenty-eight and living in Los Angeles.

FiSH! STiCKS

As Rhonda and Will settled into their booth and ordered, Will studied his wife closely. He knew something
was really bothering her. His nickname for her was "Happy
Face," because she was one of the most upbeat people he
knew. She could have a cranky service-person showing her
pictures of family members minutes after their first words.
Today was unusual, for her mood was clearly dark.

"Forget our Sunday rule, Rhonda. Do you want to talk
about what's wrong at work?"

"Will, I'm failing in my new job."

"I'm sure that can't be true," Will replied immediately.

"It is. It really is. When Madeleine left and I was promoted, I tried not to let myself worry about whether I
could live up to her remarkable example. Madeleine was
my idol; I worshiped that woman. She brought life to a dis-
mal hospital ward, a place where nobody wanted to work
because of the dreary atmosphere and lethargic people,
and she helped it become the crown jewel of Good Samaritan. We still have bigshots coming from all over the hospital and even from other hospitals to study our success.
Madeleine helped us see that the sixth-floor neuro ward
didn't need to be an unpleasant and uninviting place; that
we could make it a better place to work and a much better
place to be a patient. And with her leadership we did.

"I remember so clearly the old days, before Madeleine

5

became head nurse on the ward. I dreaded going to work even though I have always loved nursing. I had tried to maintain my usual positive attitude but it was hard. Every night when I came home, I was mentally and physically exhausted. You remember.

"Then, one day, Madeleine was promoted and immediately caught our attention by showing us a film and passing out a book for us to read. The title was so odd, we thought she was joking. She used the principles in that film and book to help us see how we could create a better place to live at work."

As Rhonda paused for a bite of her meal, Will asked, "Isn't a key word in that story 'we'? Didn't Madeleine really rely on *you* to help her? Weren't you two all alone in your beliefs for a while?" Will remembered Rhonda's frustration with her coworkers, who were deeply suspicious of any attempt to influence them. "Just another program," they said. "This too will pass." And the famous, "Been there, Done that, and Got the T-shirt."

Rhonda finished chewing and picked up the conversation. "That's true, but I can't blame the others for being wary. Health care has had so many changes that people have become cynical and resistant to being jerked around again. Once everyone realized that this wasn't just another program but more of an invitation to team up and create something really cool, then the energy started to build pretty quickly. It wasn't long before people in other parts of the hospital took notice. Madeleine became kind of a celebrity. We joked that she started a positive 'staff infection' of joy, caring, and compassion. That's when she began to help other parts of the hospital system, and that's why they asked her to become a consultant to hospitals all up and down the East Coast."

"Rhonda, I know all that. I know she's a dynamo; but so are you. She gives you a lot of credit, you know. And she told everyone she has total confidence in your ability to take over from her running the neuro ward."

"I know, I know. And I believe I did make a real contribution. But now that I have her job, I'm beginning to wonder if I can keep the energy going. This week I started to doubt that I can."

"Something happen?"

"There's an aide I hired just three weeks ago, named Juan. Well, yesterday Juan told me he liked what we were doing in neuro, but just didn't feel a part of it, and so he asked me to help him get a transfer. Will, he is just the kind of competent, caring aide we need on our ward, and he doesn't want to stay! I must be doing something terribly wrong. We have had attrition before, but it has been two years since we lost someone to another unit. We still have a waiting list of people who want to come to work on six. But this seems like a warning that we are reverting to old ways. And there are other things that worry me."

"Such as?"

"Some things are hard to describe, but you can feel the difference in energy level on the ward. I don't hear quite the spirit in the nurses' voices. And the call lights seem to be staying on longer and longer before anyone responds. You don't see nurses offering to help other nurses as often, and when there is a nasty task to do the staff seems to evaporate.

"Last week a patient with a morphine drip vomited, and I just happened to be the first person to walk past his room. After I pressed the call button for him, it was ages before anyone came to help me get him cleaned and in a new gown."

"I get the picture, darling. But you have to admit you have really high standards. Perhaps this is just a momentary thing. You have some new staff and a couple nurses out on maternity leave, so it might take a bit to get the new people up to speed."

"I hope you're right, Will. What is hard for me is that

I have been entrusted with something that was working and now it is not working quite as well. It feels like a personal failure."

A Good Samaritan Monday Morning

The sixth floor was swirling with activity as Rhonda opened the stairwell door and headed for the break room, which contained a coffee machine and a refrigerator used mostly to keep brown-bag meals fresh. As she entered the break room, she acknowledged each of the three people there with a warm "Good morning." Two responded cheerfully. Juan, who was sitting by himself, barely glanced up. *What's going on with Juan?* she thought.

Rhonda then walked from the break room toward her office. On the way there, she passed a number of patient rooms. Two had blinking lights over the door so she stepped into the first to find that Mrs. Swanson simply needed a glass of water. The light over the second door was still blinking when she extricated herself from a very chatty Mrs. Swanson, but as soon as she approached she could see that there were two nurses standing in the room. The beds were occupied by a quiet and rather shy woman named Lois Anderson and her roommate, who must have come in during the night and who was sleeping fitfully.

The two nurses seemed to be discussing a game show and showed no awareness of Lois or the call light. As Rhonda entered the room with a quiet but pleasant "Good morning," the two nurses looked at her with startled expressions.

"Good morning, Rhonda. Did you see the new *Survivor* episode on TV last night? You wouldn't believe the gross stuff they had to eat."

"I am sure I wouldn't," Rhonda replied. "But are either of you aware that Lois's call light is blinking?"

In unison they looked over at Lois, who mumbled, "I need help going to the bathroom."

As one of the two nurses stammered a sheepish, "I'll help you," the other started backing out of the room. Rhonda followed.

"What was that all about, Rob?"

"Sorry, Rhonda. We both watch every episode of *Survivor* and we just got caught up in a discussion about it. It was really extreme."

"In a patient's room, Rob?"

"Not too bright, huh?"

"I'm bothered by your use of a patient room for any

conversation that doesn't involve the patient. And particularly by a conversation about, as you put it, 'gross stuff.' Lois was waiting for help, and you didn't even know that—even though you were in her room. This just isn't the kind of environment we've said we want to create."

Just then, Paul, one of the hardest working orderlies, came up behind them pushing a gurney with a middle-aged man on it. Two bottles were suspended on hooks above the gurney.

"Good morning, Paul. Is this a new patient or a transfer?"

"Mr. Abbot was released from the ICU this morning after a week there. I'm taking him to room 614. There was that accident on the George Washington Bridge last night and the victims were brought to us. I think Mr. Abbot would have spent another day in the ICU otherwise, but they needed the beds."

"I hear you, Paul. We'll need to stay extra alert with Mr. Abbot."

Rhonda spoke into the ear of a mostly unresponsive Mr. Abbot. "We are going to take good care of you here, Mr. Abbot. I'll be down later to see how you are settling in."

Rob had slipped away as she was talking with Paul.

When Rhonda stepped into her office, she was met by the sound of a ringing phone. For the rest of the day the action was nonstop. There were bed shortages, nurses out sick, supply mistakes, families to greet, staff who just needed to talk, grand rounds, training to be scheduled, and on and on. It was well into the afternoon before Rhonda had a chance to think more about her problem and another incident that brought it to mind.

Rhonda was approaching the nurses' station in the center of the sixth floor, where the three wings converge and the elevators are located. She overheard a conversation that reminded her of the old days. Marge, a hard-edged nurse with twenty-five years' experience, was in the process of briefing Beth, a young nurse who had quickly become a leader on the floor. Beth was just beginning her shift.

Rhonda could hear Marge saying, "This guy in 614 is a real pain in the butt. Why didn't they keep him in ICU for another day? His call light is on all the time, and when you go down there you can't understand what he is saying and then he gets all frustrated. This job is hard enough without that crap. Look out for him." Marge then stormed off.

"Hello Beth—was Marge talking about our new patient, Mr. Abbot?"

"Rhonda. I didn't see you come up. I was just getting briefed by Marge on a problem."

"Does the problem happen to be a patient with a name, Beth?"

Beth's mouth dropped open and her face took on a crimson glow. Then she smiled and said, "Busted."

"You're a leader here, Beth, and I don't want to make too much of such a rare slip, but I have a larger concern. Help me understand what's happening if you can. You were the first one to embellish your identification badge to demonstrate your commitment to our new approach to nursing on the sixth floor. And you were there when we saw how our work-lives and the quality of patient care might improve if we brought a lighthearted energy to our work. You were in the front of the pack when we made the choice to be present for our patients and for each other. Now, all over the hospital, you can see other departments following our lead. You were one of a small core that made the early commitment on this floor. But here on six, the place it all began, we seem to be losing it. Is it just me, or is something happening?"

"I really hadn't noticed, Rhonda. You know how excited I am about what we have here. I really look forward to coming to work in the morning. That in and of itself makes it worth the effort. I don't always enjoy the work I am doing—bedpans and IV drips are not enchanting objects. But I always enjoy the way we work together and the way we provide care.

"That story about the fishmongers being fully present for customers really hit home with me, and I saw the implications for my work with patients. But you know, when things get stressful I sometimes forget about the possibilities and simply put my head down and plow ahead. And things are really stressful right now. All the rooms are full and many of the patients require a lot of care. Some of us are totally worn out from the sheer volume of work. Perhaps we have lost our focus, but please understand: I'm not any less positive about what we have created."

"Do you remember what you said about our new way of nursing on six? Do you remember how you framed it?"

"I'm not sure what you are referring to, Rhonda."

"You said as nurses here we always took great care of the *physical* needs of our patients, but that it was time we recognized that our patients bring their *soul and spirit* along with their body. I don't know if I ever told you how much that comment touched me. We have to find a way to hang on to the progress we've made. Our patients bring their soul and spirit with them, Beth, and so do we! If we fall back now, *we* lose out as well."

"We can't fall back, Rhonda. I was drawn to nursing to be that kind of a nurse. But it's hard to remember all this stuff that makes so much sense now, as we stand here talking calmly, when you have a day—a string of days—like I've had. You know that it has been one crisis after another, with too many things to do and not enough help. I'm exhausted and I'm really stressed out. I do want the best for our patients and for us. It's just hard right now."

"I know it's hard," said Rhonda. "I'm starting to wonder if the creation of this high-energy, fun-loving work environment was the easy part. Keeping it going is turning out to be a difficult task."

"Well at least we have something worthwhile to keep going. And we do have an investment to protect. It took a while to create, as you well know."

"You know, Beth, when you think about it, everything needs a little maintenance to keep its value. When my daughter Ann forgot to check the oil in her car she found out the hard way about the relationship between maintenance and value."

"I know what you mean. I have some family silver and I really love the connection with my past. If family members hadn't polished it regularly over the generations it would not have lasted to enhance my life. We polish it for our children and our children's children to enjoy. It takes some work to keep things you value in good shape. That holds true for silver, cars, relationships, and our work life on the sixth floor. I do want to help, Rhonda. But it's not easy. There's just so much work that needs to be done and a limited amount of time and energy."

"I know. But I'm sure we can figure this out."

Just then, Mr. Abbot's light went on. With a vibrant smile, Beth turned and strode down the hall toward his room.

A Timely Phone Call

"May I speak with Margo Carter, please? This is Rhonda Bullock."

"Rhonda, I'm so glad you called. It's been too long. How's life in New Jersey? I talked to Will yesterday. Did he tell you? How are things at work? No, don't answer that. Let's have lunch and catch up. No, let's have dinner. I discovered this neat sushi restaurant in my neighborhood and I want you to experience it. When can we meet? How about this week? What do you think?"

The minute a new way of working is initiated, the gravity pull of old ways begins.

In the beginning, novelty can be an adequate source of energy. Over time a deeper and more sustainable source must be found.

Rhonda was not known as someone at a loss for words, but her oldest friend was a talker. They had known each other since first grade at P.S. 163. After college, Rhonda had moved to New Jersey and Margo had stayed in Manhattan. "That's a great idea, Margo. I'm pretty open. When and where?"

"How about six o'clock Thursday at Takara Too on Sullivan Street. That's in the village between Bleecker and Houston. You'll know you're in the right place if you see a huge line of people waiting to get in. Dress for the weather, because we'll probably stand outside on line for a while. Got to go. See you Thursday."

Rhonda felt like she had run a four-minute mile. *Stand outside for a while; then why go there? Well, it should be interesting. Actually any time with Margo is interesting.*

Takara Too

Come Thursday, Rhonda left the kids with Will and took the Path train into Manhattan. As she walked along Bleecker Street toward Sullivan, she enjoyed the architectural and human diversity in that part of Manhattan, where Soho and Greenwich Village meet.

I forgot how alive the city is in the evening.

"So how's your new assignment? What's it like having helped create a wonderful new patient-care culture and then finding yourself in charge?"

"I don't want to spoil our dinner by talking about my work problems."

"Problems?"

"Really, Margo, I am so happy to see you and I want to catch up on all you're doing. I'm afraid that once I begin talking about my work problems I won't stop."

"Rhonda, the glue of our long friendship is the fact that we are always there for each other and can always talk about anything. What's going on at work?"

"I'm watching our wonderful new culture, as you call it, slip away from us a little at a time. And I don't know what to do. It's all coming unglued. We seem to be losing our focus as the reality of working in an active hospital reasserts itself.

"There has always been some attrition, Margo. People move, get promoted, go to school, and have families as they always have. But now there is the threat of turnover and we haven't had that for a long time."

"Great distinction! Every time we see each other you talk more like a leader. You're right. Attrition is a fact of life—people move, preferences change, promotions come—but you can have an impact on turnover."

Attrition is a fact of life.

But turnover is preventable.

"Juan, one of the new recruits, doesn't want to stay, and he is exactly the kind of aide we want and need. He told me he loves the energy on the sixth floor but doesn't feel a part of it. It's not that the staff is unfriendly. He says they have all been polite and respectful. It's just that they seem distant. This never would have happened when Madeleine was there. I appreciate your kind words about my leadership, but I'm having some doubts about being able to fill her shoes. There are other signs that the special place we've created for our patients and for ourselves is slipping away. Health care can be a sea of stress, and for a while we created an island of sanity that served as an antidote to that stress. I don't know what to do."

"Rhonda, are you aware that the problems you are facing are quite predictable? You know that if Madeleine were still in charge, she too would be facing them?"

"What do you mean?"

"Well, I have learned in my work that it is one thing to implement change and quite another to make it stick. The gravity pull of old ways starts the minute you initiate something new. When the energy is high, you aren't even aware of the pull. After you have been operational for a while, people lose some of their focus and it takes a different set of commitments and a different type of focus to keep things going. A lot of the early energy comes from things you do, external things like events. Eventually the new way of being will live or die according to the degree an internal source of energy and direction can be established."

"How do you know so much about it?"

"I have some experience with a customer-service project that provided me with a similar challenge. I'll tell you more about it over dinner, but right now I have an admission to make."

"What's that?"

"Remember I said I'd talked to Will the other day? We're here at this restaurant because of that conversation. When I called for you and you weren't in, Will wanted to talk. He told me about your struggle at the hospital. He's quite concerned, you know."

"You talked to Will about me?" Rhonda found herself a bit annoyed at first, but then realized there was nothing to be annoyed about.

"Yes, and if you hadn't happened to call me I would have called you."

"Well, do you really think this challenge would be present regardless of who was in charge? Is it like a cycle or stage you go through? I can't help thinking I'm just not up to this job."

"What you are experiencing is a very, very common problem. The good news is that there are some great examples of people and places that seem to have solved the problem. The line we are now in started forming every day four years ago. That's a very long run by New York standards. When we get inside you will meet Mrs. Ishihara, or Ishy, as she likes to be called, and her husband—if they can find a moment to say hello. They do know we're coming tonight. She has been a delightful mentor to me in my work and I have a hunch she may be helpful to you."

"You have a sushi chef as a mentor in banking."

"Absolutely! She's a great leader, as you'll soon discover. And best of all, she knows how to keep a good thing going."

"If she's a friend of yours then why are we standing in line?"

"It's part of the way she runs her business. Everyone is special here. No one gets a reservation and no one cuts the line."

"So we're here to see how she runs her business?"

"Yes. That's the reason. Ishy ran the family business in Seattle, a restaurant called Takara, but she longed to be a sushi chef. A female sushi chef is as rare as a solar eclipse, but she was determined. Her husband is a sushi chef and a real mensch. While she ran the business, he taught her the trade during their free time. When she felt she was ready, they turned Seattle Takara over to her sister and moved to New York to start Takara Too. Now she has a reputation as one of the best sushi chefs in the U.S."

"Why did she come here?"

"Why not? New York is the eating capital of the world."

The line had moved slowly and they were now in front of the awning. As they pushed aside one of the transparent plastic curtains they were greeted with a rush of warm air. Stepping inside the tent formed by the awning and the hanging plastic sheets, they gave their names to a tall waiter and then took their position behind some of New York's most diverse. In addition to the loving couple there were business suits, grunge wear, enough pierced skin to set off all the metal detectors at LaGuardia, and a Japanese family of four. The tall waiter disappeared like a puff of wind. Then he returned, handed them each a menu, and pointed out the specials, which were printed in small, delicate calligraphy. Margo handed the menu back to Rhonda, saying, "I left my reading glasses at work, so you'll have to read it for me."

The tall waiter smiled and took Margo's menu back from Rhonda. As he softly moved away, everyone stepped back to allow a number of smiling customers to exit the restaurant. And then the tall waiter was back again, holding a beautiful silver tray with six pairs of loaner reading glasses arrayed and marked according to power, weakest to strongest. Margo seemed genuinely surprised, but quickly took a pair of the strongest glasses and thanked the waiter warmly as he once more handed her a menu. She looked at Rhonda, who was watching all this intently, and said, "Always something new here."

Soon, a soft voice said, "Your table is ready."

As they moved into the restaurant, they were met with an enthusiastic Japanese hello and a burst of applause from the entire staff. It was both an exciting and welcoming greeting, and it created a sense of anticipation, perhaps even adventure.

They scrunched into two seats at the end of a row of tables closest to the counter where the sushi was being prepared and quickly smiled at their neighbors—not characteristic New York behavior, but the atmosphere was so intimate it seemed natural. In fact, it generated a couple of return smiles. Behind the counter on a slightly raised platform were four sushi chefs working with quick, controlled movements. They shouted to each other as they prepared the sushi, pausing only to applaud new customers. White stucco, hanging blowfish, hand-lettered signs, a silk-screen tapestry, exposed heating pipes, clean but well-used tables, and not an empty chair in the room—that was the decor. And it was easy to spot Ishy since she was the only woman behind the counter, and she smiled and winked at Margo as they sat.

"Well, what do you think of Takara Too?"

Before Rhonda could answer, a waiter appeared. When they gave him their attention, he asked if they had a drink preference or any questions. They ordered tea and looked at the menu. Then Margo looked up at him and said, "Why don't we turn it over to Ishy?" He smiled his approval. Standing nearby, Ishy chuckled.

Rhonda confided to Margo: "I know sushi is very popular, but I generally prefer soul food and Diet Dr Pepper."

"Trust me—it won't be too unusual and there will be plenty of choices."

"That's fine. Don't worry about me."

The waiter returned with the same calm presence Rhonda had noticed in the demeanor of the tall man at the door and deftly placed the tea on their table. Then he

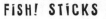
set a Diet Dr Pepper in front of Rhonda, who looked up startled and received a bright smile and a nod.

"I know you don't have that much experience with sushi," said Margo. "But this visit is not about the food, although anything that is served here is of the very highest quality."

"So we're here to meet Ishy?"

"Yes, but that's based on some assumptions I made after talking with Will. If I was wrong, we'll simply have a great meal and catch up. If my assumption was correct, we'll do all of that and meet a remarkable woman who has discovered for herself the keys to sustaining a successful work culture.

"Ishy really saved me when I ran into a problem at the bank, the same kind of problem you now have. I had taken the lead in establishing a new customer-service initiative and it worked so well that we were starting to receive recognition not only within the bank but also from the whole banking profession. I know I bent your ear more than once about that three years ago."

"Oh, that program. Didn't you call it WOW or something like that?"

"Yep. Good memory."

"So what happened to WOW?"

"Well, it all began to unravel at the very same time the bank recognized our work by nominating me for a city-wide leadership training program. You can imagine how stressful and embarrassing that was. I was being honored for something that was, at the same time, falling apart."

"I was a floor nurse then, and remember thinking that management is definitely not for me after I saw what you were going through. Now all I can think is that I should have remained a floor nurse."

"You'll do just fine, Rhonda. If ever there was a natural leader it's you. Anyway, it was in the city-wide leadership program that I met Ishy. Ishy has a way of doing business that keeps people coming back and makes them eager to tell others about their great experience here. Ishy, her husband, and the rest of the crew here have a formula for sustaining their vision for a great sushi restaurant and they are doing it in the most competitive market in the world."

"What's the recipe?"

"Not so fast, Rhonda! Let's just experience Takara Too and then let Ishy set the context. Although I have read many books on the subject, what I know about getting a vision to stick in a real organization with real competitors comes from her."

With that, the first course arrived.

"Ms. Bullock and Ms. Carter, your broiled yellowtail collar," the waiter said as he set a massive piece of fish on the table. "It's good to see you again, Ms. Carter, and I hope you enjoy your first visit to Takara Too, Ms. Bullock. I'll leave you alone between courses unless you remove the small piece of sushi from this pedestal. You can eat it or just remove it and I'll know you need something." He placed a delicate piece of sushi on the miniature pedestal that graced their table.

"Thank you. May I ask you a question"—Rhonda glanced at his name tag—"Tako?"

"Certainly."

"How did you know I wanted a Diet Dr Pepper?"

"I heard you mention it. I can take it back if you don't want it."

"I was dying for a Diet Dr Pepper! Thank you. But I didn't see it listed on your menu under beverages."

"That's because we don't stock it. But there's a deli a block from here that does carry it and I needed the exercise. I hope you enjoy it." The waiter smiled and then went to help a busboy clean an area of a table that had just been vacated.

"Now," said Margo, "let's get down to the business of

eating. This is the neck of the yellowtail tuna. It's a real delicacy. Grab those chopsticks and give it a try."

"Wait a minute. How did he know my name?"

Margo grinned and responded, "Remember when we were in line the host came over and greeted us?"

"Yes, he took down our names. He also repeated them to see if he pronounced them correctly. I thought that a bit unusual, but I now see the name was passed along to our waiter. When do they do that?"

"I don't know, but it happens seamlessly every time."

They were soon immersed in a sea of wonderful tastes and textures that didn't end until the last piece of sushi was presented and eaten. At one point during the meal their waiter pulled up a camp stool and sat down with them. He didn't ask them if everything was OK, but instead engaged them in a conversation about the sushi. It felt unhurried even though it only lasted a minute.

Vision Moments

"Do you like the sushi?" Rhonda and Margo looked up from their conversation to see Ishy standing by the table.

"It was wonderful, Ishy; I want you to meet my friend

Rhonda. I told you a little bit about her work at Good Samaritan when I called you."

"Welcome to Takara Too, Rhonda. I only have a few moments right now, but I wanted to say hello and tell you I'm available to offer whatever help I can. Margo and I had some fun a couple years ago dreaming up ways to help her bank. I'm sure that preparing sushi and operating a restaurant is much less complicated than health care, but Margo seems to think some of the things we do to stay fresh might be helpful. Do you have any questions?"

"How do you keep people standing in line for four years?"

Ishy broke into a massive smile and said, "One 'vision moment' at a time."

"Vision moment?"

"We have an experience we are working to create here and each of us takes responsibility for that creation. The line of customers could disappear tomorrow for any number of reasons—we all know that. So we live as many vision moments as we can. Margo and I were in a program where they talked a lot about knowing clearly what you are trying to create and finding the vision to communicate your goals. So we call the moments that arise each day that allow us to live the vision for Takara Too, 'vision moments.'"

"I'm sure I just experienced quite a few, but the one I remember is the Diet Dr. Pepper."

"Yes, I saw that. Tako is always looking for ways to do a little extra for our customers."

"It must help to have great sushi, too."

"Absolutely! The quality of the sushi we serve is vitally important, but there are many restaurants that have great sushi. It is the quality of the experience we create for our customers that keeps the line outside from going away. And we are always looking for ways to enhance the experience."

"What is this experience you are creating?"

"You tell me. You experienced it."

"OK. I'll try, but please excuse me if I miss something important. I would say the quality of everything on the menu is a part of it. Margo tells me that if you can't find a high-quality piece of tuna, you don't serve tuna that night. Your understated and eclectic setting is a part of it. The gentle and engaging manner of your waitstaff must be a conscious thing and part of it. And there is also the sample we were graciously offered as we froze our butts off standing on line."

A vision is made manifest in real time by identifying and bringing to life possibilities that are always present. These become "vision moments" once we take action.

Ishy smiled and said, "We ran out of butt warmers just before you arrived. Go on."

"The awning shows a concern for customers and flaunts your popularity in a subtle way. The experience you create with the high-energy greetings and applause is part of it. But what impressed me the most was the un-rushed way your waitstaff interacted with us. I felt as if I could stay all night, but you turn tables with regularity. I now realize that your staff let us savor each course, but cleared immediately once we were done. They moved quickly so we didn't have to. How am I doing?"

"You can start tomorrow!" At this they had a good laugh.

Ishy looked directly at Rhonda and continued, "I meant what I said about helping, Rhonda. Let me know. You identified most of the observable features of our vision for a restaurant. The trick, however, as you might expect, is keeping this vision alive by living our individual and collective vision moments. According to Margo, you've made some remarkable changes at Good Samaritan. That's just the beginning. Now it's time for you to put in place the engine of renewal. I'd like to help you if I can."

"So do you suggest that I go back to the hospital and tell people about vision moments?"

"What I suggest is that you and Margo go for a walk and come back in an hour. We'll talk more after I've finished serving my customers. Do you have time to do that?"

Rhonda looked at Margo, who nodded. "Absolutely," said Rhonda. "See you in an hour."

A Sushi Walk

As they stood up, Ishy shouted something in Japanese. The three chefs at the counter repeated it with three grins as Ishy rejoined them. "I wonder what she said, Margo. The chefs clearly got a kick out of it."

"I think she said, 'The wicked witch of sushi returning to work.' They do crazy little things like that once in a while; it keeps life interesting."

After Rhonda called Will to say she'd be home a lot later than planned, she and Margo carefully wove their way to the exit. Rhonda suddenly felt a surge of hope. *Four years*, she thought. *Just maybe . . .*

"Let's go look at the other sushi restaurants in the neighborhood," suggested Margo. And off they went on a tour of three sushi restaurants, all within a few blocks. None of them were very busy even though it was still the peak dinner hour on the busiest weekday. One place that must have cost millions to decorate sat mostly empty.

Margo commented as they looked through the window, "They have the finest décor money can buy, but they haven't been able to create an experience that customers value. I'm sure their sushi is of the highest quality, but they don't have a clear vision. They have a world-class facility, but they haven't been able to create an environment to match.

"Rhonda, you and your staff do have a vision of what you want on the sixth floor. You have created a special experience for patients and staff, a place where the whole person can heal. The next challenge is finding a way to keep alive and vital that experience you have worked so hard to create and to keep yourselves from backsliding."

Real Conversations

Ishy was waiting for them at an empty table off to the side. A few diners were enthusiastically finishing their meals. Rhonda decided to get right to the point given the hour and the fact that they had all gone through a full day.

"If you were in my position, Ishy, where would you begin?"

"I would start with conversations about work and about IT."

"IT? What do you mean by IT?"

"Your IT is your personal piece of the vision. Organizational visions are often written in flowery and abstract language. They need to be written that way because of the many stakeholders involved. But your own IT needs to be more focused, specific, and personal. And you find IT through conversation. In fact that is the only way to find IT.

"So if your vision is a particular philosophy for health care, you find your IT by talking to others about work and about your place within that vision. By the way, I suggest you wait a while before you talk about IT around the hospital. It might actually distract people, because it does sound a bit strange at first, and you can do a lot without mentioning IT."

"You don't need to worry about me. I'm not about to go back and talk about IT before I understand it better. But let me see if I'm getting this: These conversations are about each person's own individual relationship to the special sixth-floor experience we are jointly working to create?"

"Exactly! You might start with questions like: What are *we* creating here with our precious life energy? To what are *we* committed? Then: What is *my* role inside the vision? What is at stake for *me*? You know: questions like that. Deep questions about work that will get people to pause and think about what they do and the way they do it. One of the great things about these deep conversations is that just the act of having the conversations often increases the energy level. Natural energy is released when we talk about things that are important to us. The way we live our life at work is a vital topic, and the energy that sustains change will flow from those conversations. It's a vital topic because we all are aware of the huge amount of time we spend at work."

"I think I experienced something like this earlier this week," said Rhonda. "I started off reprimanding a terrific employee who made a mistake. We wound up having a real conversation. And just that conversation seemed to help her regain her energy.

"May I come back and talk with you again? This feels like an important place to start, but it also feels like the tip of the iceberg."

A quick hug at the station and a promise to talk again soon, and Rhonda was on her way home. On the train she took out a small pad and wrote down a few things. *So much to remember,* she thought.

The only way to find our IT inside the vision is to talk about work with coworkers.

These conversations must be both real and fierce.

Real because they require an authenticity that belies pretense or posturing.

Fierce because the amount of time we spend at work makes these conversations vital to a satisfying life.

Friday flew by and the weekend was one continuous shuttle service for the kids and a long conversation with her stepdaughter, Ann, in LA. The bond between Rhonda and Ann had always been strong and grew stronger each year. Rhonda always felt some sadness after talking with Ann because she so missed having her with them in New Jersey. But she felt less sadness after this call because they were making plans for Ann to come home for a visit.

Contemplating the Week Ahead

The children were in their rooms studying and Rhonda was thinking about work again. She took out her notes from the ride home from Takara Too and reviewed them.

Notes from Dinner with Margo at Takara Too

>✖ Margo says that even if Madeleine were still head nurse on six there would be a need to replace the dependency on external energy with a more natural energy. You can only rely on external energy in the beginning.

🐟 The gravity pull of old habits begins the minute a change is made.

🐟 Ishy has sustained the popular Takara Too experience for four years.

🐟 Ishy is willing to help me with my challenges at Good Samaritan by teaching me more about how they sustain their vision.

🐟 It starts with real conversations.

🐟 The idea of vision moments is intriguing.

🐟 The Diet Dr. Pepper incident was Tako living a vision moment. The reading glasses were also a vision moment.

🐟 We talked about finding our IT inside the vision, but I am not sure I would feel comfortable talking to others about IT.

🐟 The one thing I can do immediately is to start real conversations with the staff at work. I can begin with questions like:
   1) What are we working to create on six?
   2) To what are we committed?
   3) What is our personal role inside the vision?
   4) What does success look like?

5) How will we support each other in keeping from backsliding?

➤ So I need to start the conversations. It is a place to begin in what will surely be a long journey to hold on to the changes we have made at the hospital.

She put the notes aside for the night, remembering a commitment that she and Ann had made to each other. They vowed they would take some time, no matter how short, for themselves each week. Rhonda realized it was now or not at all.

Ann had given her the complete works of poet David Whyte for her birthday, and she decided to read some of her favorite poems before herding Mike and Mia to the bathroom.

I am fascinated by this man's work. Imagine: a poet who takes his poetry into organizations.

Tonight one poem caught her attention and she read and reread it.

The Journey

BY DAVID WHYTE

Above the mountains
the Geese turn into
the light again

painting their
black silhouettes
on an open sky.

Sometimes everything
has to be
enscribed across
the heavens

so you can find
the one line
already written
inside you.

Sometimes it takes
a great sky
to find that

small, bright
and indescribable

wedge of freedom
in your own heart.

Sometimes with
the bones of the black
sticks left when the fire
has gone out

someone has written
something new
in the ashes
of your life.

You are not leaving
you are arriving.

I am arriving. I am arriving at a new place, a place where none have traveled before in quite the same way and where a unique challenge awaits. I have everything I need but no guarantee of success. We have a good thing going at Good Samaritan and it must be maintained and renewed. Failure is assured if no action is taken. So I will start the real conversations or, as David Whyte would surely suggest, the fierce conversations about the one life that is uniquely ours to live at work.

The First Conversations

"Good morning, Ping."

"Hi, Rhonda. What are you doing in the break room? I hardly ever see you in here taking a break."

"I guess I'm doing what I should have done when I was first promoted. I'm trying to talk with the people who do the work. Ping, I'm interested in your view of what we're trying to create on this ward. Do you mind if we talk for a minute while you drink your coffee?"

"Are you having a problem with my work, Rhonda?" Ping sounded defensive and a bit annoyed.

"Oh, no, Ping. I'm not trying to sneak up on a criticism. Your work continues to be a model for us all. I'm trying to start a conversation that is a bit awkward and unusual. What I want to do is to talk about the work we do and what it means to us. You know: have a real conversation about our work life."

Ping relaxed visibly. "That would be cool, Rhonda. Just give me a second while I get another cup of coffee. Can I get something for you?"

"I'm fine, thanks."

"You want to know my view of what we are creating on the floor. Tell me again exactly what you want to find out?"

FISH! STICKS

"I'm curious about what you are thinking about as you do your work during the day. You're a great nurse, Ping, and you're also fun to work with. What guides you?"

"Thanks. I've always tried to be a *good* nurse, but when Madeleine first got us talking about our choices, I realized I had the opportunity to be a *great* nurse in the same amount of time. And I really do try to maintain a lighthearted demeanor. There are enough people in the hospital who wear their underwear really tight, if you know what I mean?"

"Yes, I've noticed," said Rhonda with a chuckle.

"I also try to really listen to our patients when I'm with them. I try to be 100 percent present during those moments. And I look for little things to do that will make the day brighter for my teammates. I believe I write a key part of my life story at work and I want to write the best story I can."

"Have you noticed that we seem to be losing some of the energy we developed while Madeleine was here?" Rhonda ventured.

"Now that you mention it, Rhonda, yes, I have. It's probably normal, isn't it? I mean nothing lasts forever, does it?"

"Is that what you want?"

"Oh, no! I find working this way so much more satisfying. Before we turned things around I wanted a transfer to the ICU. I also had my resume out to other hospitals. A couple weeks ago Mercy Hospital called me about an opening in their ICU and even offered a signing bonus. I said no because I really don't want to leave. I have an investment here and I love working with this team. Well, most of the team. I definitely don't want to go back to the old boring, bickering, unconscious way we used to work. No way. You remember what it used to be like."

"I sure do, Ping."

"I'll never forget the moment I realized things had to change. I was working with a patient shortly after Madeleine showed us that film about the Seattle fish market. I was changing a dressing, the task I had gone into the room to perform, but continued talking to Heather, who was still in the hall. I happened to look up at the patient and I saw my distraction painted on his face. I decided then and there to be fully present for patients; that the quality of their experience with us is always at stake. But that was only the beginning."

"Go on, Ping."

"I don't know how to say this exactly, but something

happened as I became more and more successful at pushing aside distraction and being fully present in what I was doing. I found my life more satisfying. I was a lot less anxious. What started out as a specific insight about patient care turned into insight about the quality of my whole work experience. I know we have a lot at stake here, Rhonda."

"That's all music to my ears, Ping. Do you mind if I share your story with others here?"

"Sure, Rhonda, but please don't mention my name. That's not what it's about."

"What did you mean, though, when you said you liked working with 'most of the team'?"

"Some of the new people don't seem to get it."

"Do you mean like Juan?"

"You said it. Juan just doesn't fit in."

"Have you ever talked to Juan about what we are trying to create on this ward and why?"

"No. Isn't that a job for management?"

"I'm management now, and if there is something I should have been doing then I've dropped the ball. If we lose Juan, as I fear we might, I think we will have lost someone who could be a great asset. I was in the group that interviewed him; his last employer raved about his energy and enthusiasm. I will do what I can to correct the problem, but I'd really appreciate it if you could take some time to give Juan your perspective and maybe ask him some questions about what he wants in life. If you don't mind, I think it would be great if you could seek out not just Juan but also a couple of our other teammates and have a conversation kind of like the one we are having. I have a couple questions I'm going to use to guide me as I continue to do the same thing."

"Sure. I'm happy to do that. And I would love to know your questions."

"Okay, here they are: What attracted you to health care? What is the Good Samaritan experience we are working to create for patients and staff on the sixth floor? What is our individual contribution to that experience? What is at stake for you?"

During the week, Rhonda hung out in the break room as much as she could. She came early to see the night staff and left late so she could spend some time with the second shift. None of the old-timers wanted to go back to the way things were; they liked the energy on the floor. But the new hires with whom Rhonda spoke said they still felt like outsiders. And no attempt had been made to integrate the three temporary replacements. The temps had been well briefed on their assignments, but no one had bothered to say anything to them about the shared vision for work on the floor.

On Thursday she found Juan alone in the cafeteria and stood next to him with her tray. "Hello, Juan. May I sit with you or would you rather be alone during lunch?"

Juan seemed startled by the question and her presence, but made a welcoming gesture with his arm. "Please join me. I just got here."

Rhonda sat down and they ate silently for a minute or two. Rhonda then broke the silence with, "Have I told you how much you impressed the selection committee?"

"No. That's nice to hear. When I moved to New York after my wife's promotion I had offers from a number of hospitals. This place had my kind of energy. I was surprised it didn't seem to be working out for me."

"Didn't seem to be working out?"

"Well, I felt like an outsider after I got here. You had the toys and posters and stuffed fish everywhere and I wasn't a part of all that. The staff seemed to be having a good time, but it didn't include me. All the neat stuff happened before I arrived. I had a talk with Ping yesterday and I am still in a state of shock. Good shock."

"Oh?"

"She and I had a real 'man-to-man' conversation. You

know what I mean. And I told her I didn't feel a part of things and she told me I came off as aloof. Wow! That stung. But I can sort of see it from her perspective."

"So what are you thinking?"

"Well, I've decided to talk to some other people so I can better understand what makes this place tick. It feels good to be taking more responsibility for how I fit here. I guess it's a two-way thing."

"Let me know if I can be of help."

"Sure, Rhonda. And thanks for telling me that stuff about the selection committee. I needed that."

An announcement interrupted their conversation. "Rhonda Bullock, please report to the sixth floor."

"Got to go, Juan. Duty calls." Rhonda saw a line at the elevator and took the stairs to six where she found a number of nurses using their lunchtime to sing to patients. They wanted her voice and she gladly gave it.

Surprise!

A few weeks had passed since her dinner with Margo at Takara Too, and Rhonda continued to have and encourage conversations about work with the staff. No one was really sure why, but the conversations were having an impact and some of the old energy was returning. But life was about to intrude.

"Good morning, Rhonda. This place is colorful."

Rhonda turned to find Phil, the hospital director, standing with a tall woman wearing a starched white uniform complete with an old-fashioned white nursing hat. "Good morning, Phil."

"I would like you to meet our new vice president of nursing, Mable Scallpell. Headquarters has assigned her to us. As you know, the position has been open for quite a while, and I'm happy to have it filled by someone so qualified."

"I'm please to meet you. How would you like to be addressed?"

"Call me Miss Scallpell, if you don't mind."

"Well, I'll leave you two to get acquainted," said Phil as he quickly backed away.

"Thanks, Phil," said Rhonda to his back as he moved hurriedly away. "So where were you before, Miss Scallpell?"

"For the last fifteen years I've been VP for research. It feels so good to get back to patient care one more time before I retire. This hospital has such a great reputation at Headquarters."

"Well, that's good to hear."

"But isn't all this commotion a little disturbing to patients?"

Rhonda felt herself tighten up a bit. "Commotion?"

"The colors, the little plastic fish on the name badges, the toys, the stuff on the wall. I'm sure it distracts people from caring for the patients."

"Actually, our patients seem to appreciate our efforts. And the fish stuff reminds us of the story of the fish market where the employees play; choose their attitude; are truly *present* at work; and make each customer's day."

"I think you should ditch the toys and signs."

"But . . ."

"It's decided. It may be the first decision I've made on this job, but I think it's an important one. I want you to tell your nurses that we are going to do things differently. Get back to a more professional way of nursing. The silly name badges must go. The toys must go. They're just not professional. You might even think about wearing a real nursing uniform like mine. Any questions?"

"Well, I . . ."

"You are new on your job. Not quite a year, right?"

"Yes but . . ."

"You will see it's for the better. I want a report each

week, and you can bring it to my office on Monday morning. We'll talk about your progress then."

You've Got to Be Kidding

"I'd like to see Phil, please."

"He's on the phone. Would you like to make an appointment, Rhonda?"

"I'll wait, thank you."

"I'm not sure when he will be available. Can I . . ."

"Hello, Rhonda," said a very sheepish-looking Phil as he came out of his office. "Come in for a minute."

Rhonda seated herself and got right to the point. "Phil, you knew, didn't you? I could see it on your face. Miss Scallpell is everything we have committed not to be. She has so much starch in her white uniform that if she fell asleep while standing she wouldn't fall over. If you take two 'l's out of her name, it cuts like a knife. You have to be joking. Not now, of all times, just when we are getting back on track. I . . ."

"OK, Rhonda, slow down and let me try to explain. My support for your efforts and the patient-care revolution we have experienced continues. Unfortunately, I do not run the Good Samaritan Hospital System, just this hospital, and this is a system-wide move. Miss Scallpell has the qualifications for the job. She really does want to get back into patient care at the end of her career. There may be some rough edges because she has been away from the hospital setting for a while. But she was a great nurse and is a great administrator."

"Rough edges! She wants me to stop doing anything fun. Too much color, she says. Unprofessional, she says."

"I know it will be a challenge, Rhonda, but hear me out. Miss Scallpell is not unreasonable. I know she wants what is best for the patients."

"One of the reasons I'm so upset about this is that since taking over from Madeleine I've observed a gradual loss of energy and a return to old ways of doing things. We've been working on the problem and we are just starting to make some progress. Now this! She wants us to remove all of the posters, all the toys, all of the visual reminders of what we are about."

Phil shrugged. "Do the best you can, Rhonda. But I'm telling you that Miss Scallpell will be our vice president of nursing for the next eighteen months and will have my full support as long as she has patient care and the well-being of staff as her highest priority. I would like you to make this work. Is that clear?"

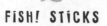

"Clear as a bell, Phil. Is the execution at dawn?"

"Cute, Rhonda. I do have one piece of advice. I mean, after all, I am the hospital director and as such I have taken credit for most of the great things done by the nursing staff here."

"Cute, Phil. What is your advice?"

"Try to understand where she is coming from and to see the world through her eyes. And when you are dealing with someone who spent a large portion of her life doing research, use facts, figures, and findings to make your points. I'm already late for a meeting, but I wanted to take this time because I know you have been caught by surprise and I feel some responsibility for that. But I also want you to think about one more thing. If the whole new changed atmosphere really depends entirely on some toys, badges, and posters, then did we really make a significant lasting change for ourselves and our patients? Or did we just redecorate?"

Word Travels Fast

Almost immediately the new regime of Mable Scallpell was the topic of discussion everywhere. In fact, on the elevator ride, one of Rhonda's favorite doctors expressed his support for Rhonda and then, as he rushed out of the elevator door on five and headed down the hall, shouted over his shoulder, "Fight for what you have created, Rhonda. The sixth floor is a great place to work and the perfect environment for patients to heal in."

The first thing Rhonda heard as she arrived on the sixth floor was a nurse saying, "We will revolt. She can't do this to us. We have worked too hard!" And that was still exactly the way Rhonda felt. Recognizing the need for some time to herself, she went to her office and shut the door.

As she sat at her desk, her eyes were drawn to her notes from Takara Too.

> . . . you can only rely on external energy in the beginning. . . . you need to replace the external energy with a more natural internal energy. . . .

What's external and what's internal? The posters may be on the wall, but they also remind us of what we are about. Do we actually still see them, or are they now a part of the background? Have we become too accustomed to the fish?

Miss Scallpell may have a point. It might be time to move away from our dependence on "crazy hat day" and all the theme stuff. But how will I ever convince the staff that this isn't one giant step back?

Rhonda decided to hold some small group meetings and to take a positive approach. At the first meeting, she briefly explained the desires of their new boss and then quickly reiterated her hopes for the conversations she had initiated. "I am very encouraged by the conversations we have started having about work," she said.

"What about Miss Scallpell?" chimed in Chelsie with the question that was on everyone's mind. "What does she think about our conversations?"

"She will also benefit from the work we do."

"No, I mean, won't she try to stop us? Talk about stiff!"

"I think we should avoid jumping to conclusions and also avoid discussing someone who isn't present. I caught myself doing that the other day and it's something we said we wouldn't do on six. It creates a negative environment. I plan to take any issues I have with Miss Scallpell directly to her and not to a third party. We need to extend to her the same courtesies we have committed to extending to each other." There were a number of nods.

"What we are doing is good for patients and good for us. We know that because we were here during the transformation to a more human and lighthearted way of nursing on six and we have seen what we started spread to other parts of the hospital. And one thing Miss Scallpell shares with us is a dedication to good patient care."

During the second of these meetings the first question was again about Miss Scallpell. Then Ping signaled she had something to say.

What is Ping doing? Rhonda thought. *I need her support here.* "Yes, Ping."

"Rhonda, I've been thinking about the challenge issued by Miss Scallpell and the investment we've made in this workplace. The conversations you started have gotten me to thinking about what a tragedy it would be if once we created a great place to work, we then let it slip away."

Here we go again. Is Ping going to ask me to fight for the colorful posters and fish?

"We have all contributed to the improvements in our work life and patient care, and therefore we have a lot at stake. But I can't help but wonder if Miss Scallpell's reaction might not be an opportunity in disguise."

"An opportunity, Ping?" There was a disbelieving buzz among the others, but Rhonda was thinking, *Go, girl!*

"Yes. I think we may have become too dependent on the external stuff, anyway. We have a fun committee. We have plastic fish attached to our name tags. We have Hawaiian shirt day. We have theme meals. And we even serve fish candy and fish crackers at our meetings— although the crackers are usually stale. I am not suggesting we give up everything that is fun, but the stuff we do doesn't have the punch it had in the beginning.

"I think we can continue doing some of the wonderful and sometimes outlandish things we do that brighten our days and delight our patients, but perhaps it is time for something more."

Beth jumped in, adding, "I've been thinking the same thing. As long as we rely on external things to keep us juiced, we are at risk. As we have just seen, the externals can be removed on the whim of a new boss. Life has a way of intruding without first asking permission. If we move the source of energy inside and take more personal responsibility for regenerating our lighthearted and service-oriented workplace, then we are more immune to some of the crazy things that can and will happen without warning. The purpose of all the stuff we did was to create a special experience for patients and staff on six. It worked, but it was a means to an end and not an end in itself."

FiSH! STiCKS

And I was worried about how to stop a riot. Sometimes I underestimate this group.

Rhonda was delighted. Two members of her staff had just summarized the primary lessons she should have just learned from Margo and Ishy. They may already have had that wisdom inside them or it may have been transmitted unconsciously during the conversations; it didn't matter. It was there.

Juan spoke up, "Why don't we put our little plastic fish inside our clothing so it's out of sight? This can be a symbol both of our dedication to keeping our way of working alive and also recognition of our personal responsibility. The fish has gone inside."

There was a short discussion about whether this was external or internal. Ping spoke up and addressed the subject herself.

"I'm cool with the hidden fish and with the stickers as long as we use them as active reminders of what we are trying to create and what is at stake if we lose it. I think we should flash our fish at patients and families as a way of showing them our approach to patient care and, more important, as a way to generate more of these conversations we have been having. They will ask us what it means and we will have to explain what we are doing in our own words. Every time we do that, we will clarify what really matters to us and recommit. Does that make sense?"

There was a general outpouring of excited agreement. Rhonda made a decision on the spot.

"You guys are fantastic. I have not shared some of the things I have been doing, although I have shared my overall concerns. It appears we all are concerned about sustaining our way of working. So I want to tell you what I have learned, and what I still hope to learn, from a sushi chef."

There were a number of open mouths when she said *sushi chef.* But she decided to continue. "I don't think we can afford the time away from work to involve everyone directly in the beginning, so I would like to suggest we form a task force of volunteers representing the different shifts and different wings."

A Team Is Formed

Rhonda was pleased that Ping, Beth, Chad, and several others volunteered to join the task force. Their first meeting was held two days later at 3:30 p.m. in the break room.

"Thanks for volunteering. I know that with workloads what they are, you are making a real sacrifice. I've arranged for one hour of overtime for those who are on the day shift and for those who offered to stay late and cover for the volunteers on the evening shift. I know it's not much, but it may buy a bad cup of coffee in the cafeteria.

"A friend introduced me to a woman who operates a sushi restaurant called Takara Too, in the city. The conversations all of us here have been having about work were her idea. She has offered to meet with a group of us on a day when the restaurant is closed to share some of the ways they maintain their unique customer experience; one that has New Yorkers lined up each night in the cold, waiting for a chance to experience it.

"Her qualifications are simple. Her family business in Seattle has been in operation since 1950. It has remained a favorite there by changing with the times but always keeping the focus on the customers. For example, when tempura started to lose its appeal and tastes changed toward sushi, they adapted without missing a beat or losing a patron. The place we will meet, Takara Too, has had a long line outside every evening for four years. I believe we can learn something about keeping our vision alive from Ishy, the top sushi chef and co-owner."

"Rhonda."

"Yes, Justin."

"It's a restaurant. We're a hospital."

"That's true. And I've thought a great deal about that. But remember where we got the idea for the way we work on six. We learned it from a bunch of fishmongers. Remember: *That's* why we've had all the fish stuff. You can't always predict where you will find wisdom. We didn't want to *be* fishmongers; we were inspired by the possibilities we saw in their life at work. By the way, does anyone know of any research done during our implementation of ideas inspired by the fishmongers?"

Heather spoke up quickly. "I'm working on my MBA at NYU and we were assigned a yearlong team research project. My team was fascinated with the program and chose to look at the changes here on our ward. We created a survey and interviewed patients and staff. We also analyzed data that is routinely collected by the hospital on subjects including turnover and length of stay. Actually, we were in the middle of collecting the second round of survey data when you were promoted."

"Really! I don't remember being interviewed or filling out a survey. I must be getting old."

"You weren't randomly selected."

"Oh. I like that explanation better than getting old. Do you have any results?"

"We have a first draft of the report. I'll get you a copy."

"How does it look?"

"Our instructor suggested the results were highly significant."

"Good or bad significant?"

"Good significant."

"That might be useful information to pass along to Miss Scallpell. Now let's do some planning."

By the time the allotted hour had passed they had agreed on a date for representatives of the team to visit Takara Too.

Sushi for Nurses

The group assembled at Takara Too and was joined by Ishy, her husband, Hiro, and one of her staff. Rhonda recognized the staff member as Tako of Diet Dr Pepper fame. Introductions were made and everyone settled in. Ishy had prepared a special hand roll for everyone. You could see that Chad, one of the male nurses on the team, was fascinated.

"This is a Special Family Roll. Here, take some, Chad. In 1950 my grandfather and grandmother and two great-aunts decided to open a restaurant. They were by nature lighthearted and caring people, and the restaurant took on those qualities as well. At first it was an extension of the family. As we became successful, we needed to add non-family members, and it was also time for my grandparents to retire. We were faced with the challenge of maintaining the place for which we had become well known. We didn't want to lose it with the retirement of my grandparents.

"My father was a physician who worked long hours, and so it was pretty much up to my mother to figure out what to do. She would go for long walks, visiting successful merchants along the way and always asking lots of questions. Over time and with many mistakes our recipe for renewal evolved.

FIND IT

"My mother realized that a high level of commitment is always present in a strong and healthy organization. She began talking with her employees about the ideals to which they were committed. She discovered they had a lot more energy during and after discussions about values and commitment. She learned that talking about their commitments served to strengthen and clarify them.

"So what are you committed to? Let's start with you,

Chad, since you seem to be especially enjoying the hand rolls."

"Am I eating too much?"

"There is an endless supply, Chad. What are *you* committed to?"

"Well, to the vision and mission of Good Samaritan of course."

"And what is that?"

"You know; the stuff on the card. I haven't memorized it or anything, but I sort of know what it is."

"That stuff on the card is written to communicate with a broad range of people. How have you personalized it?"

"I am not sure what you mean."

"How have you translated that broad vision to your own working life?"

"Well, I'm committed to being part of the quality in *quality patient care*. And I want my contact with patients to be compassionate, intelligent, thoughtful, and light-hearted, rather than stiff, distant, or distracted."

"Well said, Chad. And even though you haven't memorized the Good Samaritan vision, you've found your place within it."

"Yeah. I guess I have."

FIND IT

The most basic ingredient of any vision is the individual IT.

IT is our personalization of the vision.

Vision-sustaining energy is released as we seek to find our IT through conversation.

"Anyone else?" asked Ishy, as she began preparing spicy tuna rolls.

"I'm committed to supporting my colleagues at work," added Kathy.

"I'm committed to choosing an attitude that enhances the work environment," mumbled Justin with his mouth full.

Tako spoke up. "It might help for me to explain what happens here from my perspective. We all have different roles and we will often talk about the tasks we do and how to do them better. Most places do that, I think. What is different here is that we also talk about the experience we are working to create by the way we do our work. We think about who we are *being* while we do the work we are *doing*. I wait tables; Ishy and Hiro make sushi; and other staff members perform other functions. But while we do different things, together we create an experience by the way we engage our customers and each other in the process. We talk about how we can create a unique experience every day that will draw our customers back for more."

Ishy nodded to Tako and continued, "That is the kind of discussion you need to have frequently to keep a vision energized. A few weeks ago, I suggested that Rhonda return to Good Samaritan and start a series of deep conversations about work. I understand you have started talking

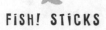

this way about work and you have already seen a change in the energy level. That's not surprising. My mother found the same thing thirty years ago.

"It's in the search for your special connection to the vision, and your conversations with each other about that connection, that your commitment becomes real. To contribute to keeping a vision alive and well you must first find your IT inside the vision. A formal vision is created for many constituencies but you draft your IT just for you. The conversations you have started support you in your discovery and rediscovery of your IT.

"You might want to consider a regular meeting where you talk about your commitments and exchange ideas about your IT," suggested Ishy. "My sister has continued to have regular meetings and frequent conversations at Seattle's Takara. And we have them every week here. It's hard to have these conversations on the fly, so you need to carve out special time together."

LIVE IT

Ishy continued. "Finding your IT is the starting point, but not enough in and of itself. More of the actual staying power comes from the next step: living your IT."

"Living it?" Mallory asked.

"Yes. So much of what happens in any thriving organization is spontaneous creativity fueled by a strong commitment to a vision. When you commit to something big, you see opportunities you might otherwise miss. You are open to them. It sounds a bit fuzzy at first, but we all commit to the vision of Takara Too and understand that we recreate it every day by the way we live at work. It is not just the work we do—which is to make and sell great sushi. It is also who we are *being* while we do the work we do."

"I'm not sure I understand what you mean by seeing things you might otherwise miss," remarked Ping.

"What I am referring to are opportunities to live the vision. But why don't I let Rhonda describe what happened the first time she and Margo came to the restaurant."

Rhonda made circles out of the fingers of her hands and held them up to her eyes like glasses. "Margo forgot her reading glasses and we were handed menus at the door. Margo returned hers because she couldn't read the small print. Literally seconds later the host was standing next to us with a whole tray of reading glasses of different strengths. It was, like, wow."

Ishy went on, "Each day we are presented with many

vision moments, or opportunities to reinforce or creatively extend our vision of the Takara experience. The more we act on these opportunities, the stronger the Takara experience becomes."

"I think I have an example from my life as a mother," said Rhonda. "I want to nourish a love of words in my children. So whenever I come upon a new word I get excited and we take some time to find out what it means. My children are now doing the same thing on their own. My stepdaughter, Ann, who had learning difficulties as a child, has developed an extensive vocabulary. The vision is to become lovers of words and the vision moments are new words that show up. It becomes an adventure."

"That's a good example, Rhonda. You've committed to raising educated children. That commitment allowed you to see an opportunity to nourish a love of words. The vision moments arise when new words present themselves and you transform the learning of these new words into adventures. Does anyone have a nursing example?"

All heads turned when the very quiet and shy Heather started to speak. "I watched Juan do something yesterday that really impressed me. We had an elderly man who came to us from ICU after a major stroke. His wife was rather creaky, needing a four-pronged cane to ambulate,

LIVE IT

Once we are clear about our IT, opportunities to Live IT are more obvious.

We call these opportunities *vision moments.*

Vision-sustaining energy builds as we live as many *vision moments* as we can.

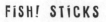

and she was planning to stay overnight with her husband. It would have been hard on her.

"Juan sat down with her and took her hand. He told her how her husband now had a larger family including all of the staff on the floor and how we were dedicated to taking good care of him. Then he turned his collar to expose a small plastic fish. He said the staff wore that fish to remind them that this man is now a special member of the hospital family and will be treated accordingly.

"She went home to her own bed, much to the relief of her son and daughter. Juan took the time to put her mind at ease and also saved the night staff from the extra work that would have come from having this woman in the room all night. I think Juan saw a vision moment."

"That's it exactly," said Ishy. "Seeing opportunities to *be* the vision leads to the recreation of the vision every day. Each of you is responsible for recreating Good Samaritan each day from scratch by the way you live there. You are it. You are Good Samaritan. So 'Live IT.'"

Ishy went on as she prepared another kind of sushi. She said, "Find IT and Live IT are critical, but without the last element of the recipe it's still just a matter of time before any vision fades. This last ingredient is both important and difficult."

Justin said, "I'm all ears."

Ishy smiled and apparently decided not to say exactly what had come into her mind. Justin did have rather large ears.

COACH IT

"Most of the time here at Takara Too we are pretty good at living the vision, but we are human, we make mistakes, and we have times where we lose our focus. That's why the final element is so critical to our overall performance. We call our method of keeping one another on target *coaching*. After all, the job of a coach is to help you do your best.

"Here, everyone becomes a coach, and any one of us can coach anyone else. It doesn't make any difference how much seniority you have or where you are on our very short ladder. In fact, I get coached all the time."

Tako leaned forward and spoke. "I was hired a couple months ago, replacing a member of the waitstaff who decided to return to Japan. During the interview process they told me about coaching and I thought to myself that I would believe it when I saw it. I was happy to have the job, so it wasn't a big thing to me, but I was curious.

"One day Ishy brought a piece of tuna back from the

market and I looked at it and saw a light discoloring that I had seen once before. Sometimes that color pattern indicates that the tuna is not really fresh. I told Ishy that, and she looked me in the eye and said, 'Look, if I didn't think it was fresh it wouldn't be served.' She spoke with an unusually harsh tone. I don't know why, but I challenged her by saying I didn't think a curt response to coaching was in the spirit of what we had discussed in the interview. I was sure I would get fired.

"Ishy actually blushed and apologized. She told me I was right and her tone was inappropriate. We then talked about my experience, and Ishy listened while I told her my theory about what happens when salt gets on the ice while fish are being transported."

Tako looked down at his feet and continued. "It's great to be able to exchange views about things that are factual or experiential. But what started as coaching about stuff became coaching about the way we treat each other and I was afraid I had stepped over the line. Now I see that the fact we can have those real conversations not only helps make this a great place to work, but it helps us create the Takara experience every day."

Ishy smiled. "Tako is being kind. My first thought when he told me the fish might not be fresh was that I have been buying fish my whole life and I certainly would not buy a tuna that was not fresh. However, I answered with an attitude that was inappropriate, even if I had been correct. As Tako coached me about my attitude, the tuna became less important because the very spirit of coaching was under the microscope. We have all committed to listening before deciding whether we will accept or reject coaching. So I listened and learned. And I think the fish was fresh."

They all chuckled at the final comment. Then Beth spoke up. "The other day I allowed the negative spirit of another nurse to affect me and I was living outside the vision for a moment. Rhonda overheard me referring to a patient in impersonal and critical terms and she called me on it. She was absolutely right. I guess I was being coached."

"You were definitely being coached, Beth. How did it feel?"

"Well, my first response was to feel a bit defensive. We work in stressful conditions and it was just one time I slipped up. But Rhonda reminded me of what we were trying to create on our floor, and I support that vision of what work can be. In a way it was about the vision, not just about me. But I did get busted!" At this Beth smiled at Rhonda, who nodded agreement.

COACH IT

Coaching is a gift we give to each other and to our vision to keep IT strong.

Whether it's about the way we do our work or the way we work together, the feedback needs to flow in all directions.

Coaching can't be an ego trip. We only do it for the vision. We Coach IT.

Ishy went on. "Coaching is evidence that you have taken your responsibility seriously, because it's hard to coach. Coaching is done by those who are deeply committed to making the place great, not just good. You demonstrate your commitment to the vision by coaching. You also demonstrate your commitment by allowing others to coach you. Coaching is the glue that holds us together and the fuel for the little corrections that keep a place burning bright. And coaching can be the stimulus for the little innovations that reinvent us.

"When you are new or are unsure of something, you need to ask for coaching. When you are an old-timer you need to share your experience by coaching. But the old-timer may have routines that keep him or her from seeing new possibilities. So when you are an old-timer you also must be open to coaching. Giving and accepting coaching is the final demonstration of your commitment to the vision. Commitment is an abstraction by itself. **Find IT, Live IT,** and **Coach IT** are the actions that make commitment real."

"Someone is pounding on the door," Chad interrupted. But by then all were aware of the knocking, and the door was opened to expose a shocked and disheveled-looking Will Bullock.

Rhonda ran to the door asking, "What is it, Will?" Will said he had news that was too awful for the phone— that he had to come tell Rhonda in person. Rhonda was immediately at his side and again, in a softer voice, said, "What is it, Will?"

Will looked at her through wet red-rimmed eyes and said, "Ann is dead." Between sobs he could be heard saying something about a car accident and a drunk driver. For a long while they just held each other. Then a friend of theirs who had been standing just outside helped them to a car that had been parked awkwardly at the curb. They drove away.

When you work at a hospital, you are familiar with death. That doesn't make it any easier when it is one of your own. In this case, all of Rhonda's coworkers and new friends were experiencing the vicarious shock of a parent's worst nightmare. They stood in stunned silence, a few silently weeping. After a while, Ping said that she was going to call the hospital. That broke the spell and they slowly drifted away to find the comfort of family and friends. Ishy remained behind, her head in her hands, her husband's hand on her shoulder.

A Parent's Worst Nightmare

We expect some day to lose our parents—but no one expects to lose a child. It violates the natural order of things. And when you are young, you give no thought at all to the prospect of losing an older sister. It was devastating for Mike and Mia. Both of them had worshiped Ann.

At the hospital the shock waves spread outward in all directions. But the reaction that surprised everyone came from Miss Scallpell.

Two hours after Ping had called with the awful news, a cab pulled up to the Bullock residence and Miss Scallpell walked up to the door. When a man with a neatly trimmed gray goatee answered she asked, "Is this the Bullock residence?"

"Yes, it is, but this is not a good time."

"Are you Will?"

"No, I'm Will's brother. Are you a friend of the family?"

"I work with Rhonda at the hospital. May I speak with her, please?"

"I'm sorry. I seem to have lost my manners. We're all in shock here. Please come in. Who shall I say is here?"

"I'm Mable Scallpell."

"Please sit down."

Mable looked around the room. It was like sitting in a photo gallery. She could quickly identify Ann. In one lovely picture Ann was standing beside a famous actor. Ann looked so vibrant in the picture.

"Miss Scallpell. What are you . . . ?"

"Rhonda, I'm here to help. I've helped out like this before"—*and it was done once for me*, she thought—"and I know what to do."

"But you don't have to . . ."

"Nurses throughout time have supported one another at times like this. You have your grieving to do and arrangements to make. I will see that the phones are manned and the table is set with food. If there is anything else you need just let me know. I'm so sorry, Rhonda. I know there aren't words, but I want you to know I am here to do whatever you need done. I have experienced loss in my life and I want to be here for you. I will stay in the background, but ask me for whatever you need."

With a *thank you* Rhonda returned to the family room, where she was sitting in shocked silence with Will. Occasionally a desperate wail would fill the air followed by uncontrolled sobbing.

I remember all too well, thought Miss Scallpell. *Something like this stays with you for a lifetime.*

Miss Scallpell went into action. In thirty minutes she had arranged around-the-clock teams of nurses to prepare food, answer the door, go to the airport, run errands, shuttle guests, make beds, do dishes, and screen phone calls. When members of the gospel choir arrived with food and offers of help, they were quickly integrated into the team. This continued until the day after the funeral, when Will and Rhonda left for a memorial service organized by Ann's friends in LA. The last thing Miss Scallpell and the volunteers did was clean the house from top to bottom.

Back at the Hospital

The work of a hospital demands constant attention, and in this case the rhythm of work was a welcome escape from the harsh reality of what had happened to a friend. When a colleague loses a child, everyone realizes that it could just as easily have happened to him or her.

A touching note was posted on the bulletin board, dictated by a six-year-old girl with a head injury—a trauma that could have been prevented with the use of a seat belt. This young girl, struggling to regain her own life, sensed something was going on and asked about it.

When she heard about Rhonda's loss she insisted on writing a note.

Dear Nurse Rhonda
    You might not remember me but I am the little girl in 611.
    I am very sorry your daughter died.
    It makes me sad.
    You must be sad too.
    I would like to give you a hug when you return.

                            Love,
                            Tena

P.S. If I have already gone home I won't be able to give you a hug.

Ping and Beth met in the hall. "You know, Beth, there are so many good people and so much kindness on this floor . . ." She couldn't finish the sentence.

"I feel it too, Ping. When something like this happens it makes you reflect on how you are living and what life is all about. We can so easily become mechanical in our work, but at a time like this our compassion comes to the surface. It feels like we become a little softer around the edges. That's why we need to keep our philosophy of work alive. That's why we became nurses: to be human. I've been thinking about Rhonda's return. I've heard it takes months before she'll have what might even re-motely be called a normal day. Maybe we need to con-tinue what was started at Takara Too. None of us wants to see a return to old ways; life is too precious to live that way at work. The best way we have to honor Ann's mem-ory is to continue what Rhonda has started. We are on the way to renewing the lighthearted, compassionate, con-scious way of working."

"You know, we spend more time at work than we do with our family and friends. We spend more time here than we spend in our places of worship. We spend more time at work than we spend in nature. The largest por-tion of our time spent awake is spent here. This is also an opportunity to test our commitment, to prove that it can be about much more than simply having more fun at work."

"Good afternoon, ladies."

"Miss Scallpell."

"I see those silly little fish are out in the open again."

"Well, we . . ."

"I may have acted a bit hastily when I first arrived. I have been looking at some data that Phil and I received from Heather and while it is preliminary, it is dramatic. You should be proud. I heard so many good things about this place when I was at the corporate office, but I really had no idea of the source of those good things. The progress in patient and staff satisfaction on this floor has been remarkable.

"But my original point remains. Are you doing anything to make sure you sustain the gains you have made— or is it just becoming a lot of distracting window dressing that hides real problems?"

"Well, we . . ."

"You know, when Rhonda comes back she will do her job and do it well, but I don't think you can continue relying on her to lead cheers."

"We were just talking . . ."

"I enjoy these talks. It's good to be back with nurses giving care. So enough chitchat, eh?" And Miss Scallpell turned to leave.

"Miss Scallpell."

She turned back to look and said, "Yes, Ping."

"Thanks for all you did. We were all wondering how to help Rhonda and her family, and you organized it all and made sure we were doing the things that were actually needed."

For the first time Miss Scallpell seemed to be at a loss for words. Her eyes began to glisten. Finally she said, "Nurses stick together, and I have had some experience with sudden loss: My husband died suddenly, many years ago. When Rhonda returns, she will not be upbeat and full of fun, but she will still be a fine nurse. There are times when melancholy is appropriate. And remember that Rhonda is on a different time line from the one we are on. Rhonda will experience intense moments of sadness for years, and that is the way it should be.

"Her grieving doesn't mean she cares less about the fun environment you have worked so hard to install here; life is not always up and she is simply being fully human. Now is your chance to prove that what you are doing here can incorporate the full breadth of human emotions and personality types—that it really is all about being committed to the patients and each other—that it's not just about fun." With that she left, pulling a handkerchief out of a heavily starched pocket as she walked away.

Beth looked at Ping. "She may be from another generation but underneath all that stiff white material is definitely the heart of a nurse."

The Memorial

Rhonda and Will arrived in Los Angeles with red-rimmed eyes and an empty feeling in their hearts. Ann's roommate, Jill, boyfriend, Rob, and friends Greg and Melissa had organized a memorial service on the beach near where Ann and Jill lived. It was a section of beach known for its regular appearance on *Baywatch* and for the dozens of volleyball courts found there.

Rhonda and Will arrived, parked their car, and looked out at the beach, where about eighty people were already standing around two blazing fire pits.

"I'm not sure I can do this, Will."

Will looked lovingly at his wife as they sat in the rental car. "You don't have to do anything, sweetheart. Do you want me to take you back to the hotel? These are her friends, they will certainly understand."

"Where do you get the strength?"

"You give me too much credit. Right now I am simply trying to get from one minute to the next. But these were her friends and I know so little about her life in the LA film business, even though she was out here for years. I want to hear about the Ann that her friends and coworkers knew."

Rhonda opened the car door and stepped out. "That's a wonderful way to approach this memorial. We will celebrate this part of her life." Rhonda took hold of Will's hand and they walked to the beach.

A Plan Forms Back at Good Samaritan

"So let's make it easy on ourselves, Beth. Let's divide into three groups based on our primary ward assignment, and each group will take one of the three principles described by Ishy. I will work with the renal wing and tackle 'Find IT,' if that's all right with you."

"That's fine, Ping. Our wing will take 'Live IT' and Chad can take 'Coach IT.'"

"How will we describe the task? I know our goal is to keep our great work environment alive, vital, and evolving. But how do we frame things?"

"Let me take a shot at that, Beth. I think our primary task is to further educate ourselves about the commitments, to share what we have learned in a fun way that involves the others, and to invite our colleagues to come up with specific ideas we can put into practice here—ways to create vision moments."

"Oh, Ping. I made some copies of the notes I took at

Takara Too. I'll brief Chad on our plan when I give him his copy. And one more thing . . . Is this OK? I mean, do you think Rhonda will mind? You know, that we are taking things into our own hands."

"Actually, I think Rhonda will be relieved. She has felt such a heavy personal responsibility for continuing what started under Madeleine's watch. I now see that we can and should take part of that burden."

There are three principles that guide Takara Too as they sustain the remarkable Takara experience.

Find IT   A vision is often designed to serve multiple constituencies. A vision comes alive only when it is personalized by those who work in the vision community. This happens when each of us assumes responsibility for finding our IT inside the vision. And we can only find our IT through conversation with other members of the vision community. The employees of Takara Too regularly take the time to talk about the place they want to create and the role each of them has in that creation.

> **Live IT**   *Every day we are presented with countless opportunities to recreate the vision. Ishy calls these **vision moments.** Once we have found our IT we must commit to living IT by living fully the naturally occurring vision moments.*
>
> **Coach IT**   *Keeping a vision alive is hard to do alone because it is difficult to observe yourself in action and feel the impact you are having on others. Therefore feedback plays a key role. By creating an atmosphere where it is not only OK but our responsibility to give and receive feedback, we will make the daily adjustments necessary to keep the vision strong. This is called coaching and it is a crucial ingredient in sustaining anything worthwhile.*
>
> **Note to self:**
> *We all must discover the power and importance of these ideas for ourselves and choose to enroll of our own free will. Natural energy comes with personal choice.*

Return to Takara Too

A month had passed since Ping and Beth had their planning conversation on the sixth floor. Rhonda had returned to work but was clearly affected by her tragic loss. She could often be seen just staring into space. It seemed to help her to be actively involved in direct patient care, and so the staff frequently asked for her help in challenging cases, for which she was now showing an even greater aptitude than she had before. Rhonda took special interest in the slow but steady progress of little Tena in 611 on the children's neurology wing; Tena's letter had a prominent place on Rhonda's bulletin board alongside a picture of Ann.

Rhonda and Miss Scallpell were briefed on the plan and were delighted. Phil had stopped by to indicate how excited he was with their effort and offered his help.

Miss Scallpell, as usual, had a lot to say. Ping, Beth, and Chad were becoming accustomed to these one-sided conversations and were actually beginning to enjoy them. It was during one of those conversations that Miss Scallpell suggested a lunch meeting to which she invited Rhonda, Ping, Beth, and Chad. They were asked to meet outside her office at 11 a.m.

"This is a bit early for lunch, isn't it?" asked Chad as he stood outside Miss Scallpell's office with Ping and Beth. Miss Scallpell emerged in a rush and they found themselves scrambling to keep up as she took off through the revolving door at the main entrance and headed for the parking lot.

"Shouldn't we wait for Rhonda?"

"She decided to cover things here for the three of you."

"That feels weird," said Chad.

"Understandable and professional," Miss Scallpell responded crisply as they marched down an aisle. "You are the team leaders, are you not?"

"Yes, but . . ."

"Enough said, hop into my car."

"Where are we going?"

"The city."

The car turned quiet as they crossed the George Washington Bridge and headed downtown. Comments were generally about the passing view. In New York, the people-watching is world class. Finally Ping asked, "So what's up for lunch, Miss Scallpell?"

"I'm an eye blink away from retirement and I spend a lot of time thinking about leaving a legacy. I am quite proud of the research programs I established for the system and thought I might coast through my last two years spreading old-fashioned nursing wisdom to a new generation of nurses. I wasn't prepared for what I found at Good Samaritan. The opportunity we have here is enormous.

"Heather's research validates what you already knew. Your efforts have had a major impact. But what I saw when I arrived was an overreliance on the externals and an inability to integrate new people. You've taught me a lot. I hope I've taught you something too. Now let's see if this much-discussed sushi chef can tell us the rest of what we need to know. Well, here we are." Miss Scallpell managed to find a parking place a short walk from the restaurant.

Ishy and Margo were waiting for them as they emerged from the car. They held open the plastic curtains used to protect those waiting in line each night from the elements.

"I can taste the sushi now." Beth was almost drooling.

Ishy smiled and responded, "Actually, we ordered corned beef sandwiches from the deli down the street. Just kidding! I have both."

They sat down at a long table and the sandwiches were passed around along with an elegant tray of sushi.

Margo spoke first. "Some of you may know that I have been active in a city-wide leadership program where I was lucky enough to meet Ishy. What you may not know is that Mable is a founder and past president of the organization."

The three nurses looked at Miss Scallpell with a mix of disbelief and respect.

"So it's not surprising that we talk to one another frequently, since what we have in common is a concern for Good Samaritan and for my oldest and dearest friend, Rhonda. Rhonda and I go back to first grade, you know.

Ishy and I want to be sure you all are getting the support you need. How are the teams doing with their assignments?"

Ping glanced at the other two nurses, who nodded, and then spoke. "Actually it isn't going well at all. We understand about the importance of finding your IT inside the vision, but we are not sure how to get started. Maybe some examples from other organizations would make it clearer.

"And we have some ideas for helping people understand 'Live IT,' and some specific vision moments to cite, but we are having trouble thinking of a way to actively engage the staff. A list of steps would be helpful.

"And, yes, 'Coach IT' is the most straightforward of the three. We know people will understand honest and clear communication because we have a tradition of feedback in health care; we have patient-care audits and medical reviews. But how do we develop a habit of choosing the same honesty and authenticity in our conversations about the way we work and who we are being at work? Again some more examples might help us."

Ishy responded, "When Rhonda went back to the hospital after our first meeting together, her plan was to begin talking to people about their work and what they wanted to get from work."

"Yes," said Ping. "I remember the day Rhonda asked if we could talk about the way we work. At first I thought I had done something wrong. That discussion led me to talk with Juan and see how we had let him down by not being more thoughtful about his need to get integrated in our way of working."

"And I understand you experienced a surge of energy as you began talking about work at a deeper level."

"It was amazing how quickly that happened."

"Well, you must have faith in that natural energy. It is always available if you can make the conversations real. And you don't really need any more examples."

"We don't?"

"I don't think so. You seem to understand the principles and you have seen how we do what we do. The time for understanding has passed and now is the time for action."

"By the way," said Miss Scallpell, "I've talked to Rhonda and she wants to get involved again, but she is concerned about stealing your thunder. She is really impressed with the way you three took responsibility and made a commitment to keep things moving. She doesn't want to interfere."

"Interfere!" Ping said. "Her interest in getting more involved in the project is the best news I've had in a long time. But let's get back to Takara Too. Can you give us some pointers on things to do to get started? Do you have like a list of things to do? I mean these ideas originated in your family business, didn't they?"

"I think I would phrase it another way," said Ishy. "Takara and Takara Too discovered the commitments needed for sustaining a vision, but we did not create them. They have been around for a long time. Ping, it's time for action.

"Your implementation strategy must be crafted in a way that respects your culture at Good Samaritan. I deeply appreciate your recognition of our efforts here, but you must find your own way of bringing this wisdom to life in your world. To spend any more time watching us or analyzing the things we do would only distract you from your real work. Your real work is to bring these commitments to life at Good Samaritan."

"We just aren't sure what to do."

"That's because your journey is unique. You may be using a set of ideas that are as old as time, but your application is brand-new and has to be discovered by you. Action in the face of the unknown requires some courage. More examples and more study is a natural but problematic form of resistance to action.

"The philosopher Joseph Campbell helped me understand. He said if you see your path laid out in front of you Step One, Step Two, Step Three, you only know one thing for sure: It's not your path. Your path is created in the moment of action. If you can see it laid out in front of you, it means you can be sure it is someone else's path. That's why you see it so clearly.

"I've learned to be open to any inspiration that comes from observing effective organizations at work, but when it comes time to take action, the last thing I need is to borrow someone else's 'how to' list. What I need to do is to take my own first step.

"We have nothing more than sushi to give you now. It is time for you to take the step that does not yet exist. You must create it."

And so they all sat at the table for another hour talking and becoming more comfortable with the inevitability of the task ahead: finding the one path that is theirs and theirs alone.

Chad and Beth walked to the subway station and left Ping and Mable to fend for themselves. They wanted to compare notes. While they were deep in conversation a store window caught Beth's attention. They stopped for a minute to study the array of family pictures on display.

Once guiding principles are understood, it is time for action.

We think we need to find the one well-worn trail that others have followed and that it will take us where we want to go.

The truth is that we must blaze our own trail and all we will ever have as a compass is a set of commitments and our faith.

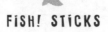

"I guess people have always captured the special moments in their life. I wonder how they did it before photography?"

"They drew pictures on the cave wall of course. What is it, Beth? You seemed to drift away there for a moment while you were looking at this display. What are you thinking about?"

And Beth shared the idea that had been stimulated by the photogaphs. Then, recognizing the deep exhaustion they both felt, they decided to take a cab all the way back.

The Commitment Gate: Find IT

On Monday morning, five weeks after Ishy issued her action challenge, the FISH! STICKS project made its first public move. In the lobby of the sixth floor at Good Samaritan, a picket fence with an old-fashioned hinged gate had been erected, but it was labeled *Commitment Gate*. Above the gate was a sign with two questions.

Are you committed to the vision of Good Samaritan?
Have you found your IT?

Off to the side was a one-chair information center and standing in front of elevators were Ping and a member of her Find IT team along with Rhonda and Miss Scallpell. As staff came off the elevator or through the door they received a big smile, a greeting, a printed card, and a silly pin.

On the back of the card was the latest version of the hospital vision statement with some new text as well.

Are you committed to the vision of Good Samaritan? Have you found your IT?

On the back of this card is a copy of the Good Samaritan vision statement. It is an important public statement of our commitment to quality health care and a great work environment, and it is written in general language for a variety of stakeholders. But it remains words on paper until you and I commit to finding our place inside the vision and bringing the vision to life through our work and through the person we are being while we do our work.

An upbeat, lighthearted, and team-based approach to work developed here on the sixth floor. The quality of our work life and patient care benefited greatly from this way of working. But now we must decide if we are committed to sustaining this

---

expanded vision of our work. Our first step must be finding our individual IT inside the vision so we can choose to live IT. And there is only one way to find our IT: through real conversations with colleagues about work.

We hope you are willing to demonstrate your commitment by having at least five conversations in the next two weeks. These conversations should provide clarity about your IT. The questions below are meant to be a starting point for each of the conversations.

> When in your workday do you know you are living the vision?

> What is the experience we are trying to create for patients and staff?

> How do you personalize the vision?

> How can we support each other in keeping our way of working alive and vital?

By 8:30 a.m. most of the staff working the day shift had seen or played with the Commitment Gate and received a smile, the greeting, the card, and the pin. The last to visit was Phil, the hospital director.

"That seemed very effective," said Phil. "But what's the deal with the pins? I thought we were moving to a more internal energy."

"We are," answered Miss Scallpell. "The external devices can only take you a certain distance and we all agree about that. But I've realized that symbols and ritual serve an important purpose in keeping a vision alive. I read about the power of symbols and rituals in a *Harvard Business Review* article about the Ritz-Carlton and I saw a connection. Let me ask you a question, Phil.

"What happens when a patient, family member, or someone from the outside sees an unusual pin on a nurse's lapel?"

"Well, I suppose that person might be curious."

"Exactly. And what happens when you begin answering their questions?"

"I get it. When you answer questions you clarify and reinforce your own understanding and your commitment. The pin assures the conversations continue by stimulating them. What else do you have up your sleeve?"

"Well, I think the Commitment Gate will be here for a few weeks. And I think we need a lost and found for those who have lost or have never found their IT. Then there is the idea that came from the planning team."

"And what would that be?"

"Where to put Miss Scallpell's starched hat, of course," Rhonda chimed in, pointing to the side of the gate, where one of Mable's hats was being hung on a special hook by Ping, Beth, and Chad. "That's a reminder to us on the sixth floor of how much Miss Scallpell has given us. Any chance you might consider delaying that retirement, Miss Scallpell?"

Photographic Memories: Live IT

The flyer announced a contest open to the staff on the sixth floor. The rules were simple. Each team would have a section of the lobby reserved for that team and a bulletin board to display photographs taken by the members of their group who were caught in the act of living their IT. These photos of vision moments would be mounted on the bulletin boards. The rules also indicated that the boards could be decorated, and that all the photos needed to be of vision moments where a hospital patient wasn't physically present. And all had to be true snapshots—not posed. The teams would have four weeks to prepare the displays. A committee of nurses from other floors would judge the results.

"Live the Vision"
Contest Announcement

All members of the sixth-floor staff are invited to participate in the first annual Live IT competition. The purpose of this contest is to identify and portray the many ways we live the vision of Good Samaritan each day by living our personal IT. You are invited to form teams based on your work assignment and to compete for the prizes.

It is the task of each team to capture spontaneous *vision moments* in photographs. *Vision moments* are those times when we are living the vision of Good Samaritan. The pictures will provide a documentary of the moments you and your team bring to life in the course of your work, and will be displayed for judging. See the detailed rules on the back of this flyer and contact Beth at 6121 with any questions.

Good luck!

First prize was on display. It was a picture of a giant tray of sushi. The real sushi would go to the winning team.

The Live IT Judging

Four weeks had passed since the contest was announced and the lobby was packed. "I hope the fire marshal doesn't show up," said Beth jokingly to Juan.

The spokesperson for the selection committee moved to the small stage that had been erected and took the microphone. Silence fell over the crowd, which included representatives from all the teams.

"Ladies and gentlemen, it is my pleasure to announce the Live IT winners and present the awards. The instructions were to create a collection of photographs depicting the many ways our vision is personalized by those who work on and support the sixth floor. It was the hope of the contest organizers that the search for the ways we live the vision, or *vision moments*, as we now call them, would make us all more aware of the opportunities we each have every moment of every day to keep our precious vision alive and full of energy. May I have the envelope, please?"

Margo stepped up and handed her the envelope. "This is Margo Carter, executive vice president of Eastern Bank Systems, where the results have been locked in the bank vault." There was polite laughter, but everyone seemed ready for the results.

"Second prize goes to the very competitive team from top management. The judges were especially impressed with the amount of 'play' that goes on in the executive suite. The vision moments where senior executives are meeting with and listening to groups of employees over lunch was also a factor in the decision. I understand they had to eat in the cafeteria because the executive lunchroom was full of pictures." There were some chuckles. "Give them a hand."

Phil stepped up to accept the prize but declined making any remarks with the quiet comment, "I don't want to detract from the main focus, but I do want to announce that the executive lunchroom will reopen as a general purpose room for everyone's use. This idea came from our own Miss Scallpell, who convinced me that doctors, nurses, and other staff often need a place to get away for a minute or two." This comment received a well-deserved hand.

"And now for the first prize. This was an easy decision for the judges. First prize is awarded to the nurse assistants and nutritionists of the sixth floor. The selection committee was impressed not only by the array of things you captured in your pictures as you do the work that is at the heart of our mission at Good Samaritan, but also by the example you set for the rest of us.

"Your collection of pictures about everything you do behind the scenes for patients made its point so clearly thanks to the clever way you approached it. We especially liked the pictures of the food trays for pediatrics with the pancakes decorated to look like Pokémon characters. It was a powerful statement of how simple it is to create a higher quality of life for those we serve just by spending a little extra time and ingenuity. You've given new meaning to the phrase, 'play with your food.' We will be displaying your pictures on a rotating basis in all parts of the hospital, and they will then go on a tour of all the hospitals. And we're even going to turn the photos into a slide-show video for the kids and staff.

"An anonymous donor has provided a gift basket for each of you. This person is doing this to demonstrate his thanks to you for the wonderful care you gave his wife while she was on six. Good job!"

Coach IT

The Coach IT team had gone underground and Chad was not talking to anyone about what they were doing. Two weeks after the vision moments were on display, Ping tracked him down.

"How is it going, Chad?"

"Just fine. Good seeing you, but I've got to run."

Later Beth encountered a shrug and a polite, "Chill out," when she inquired about the progress of the Coach IT team.

Rhonda, who was taking a more active role as time passed, was especially concerned. She knew that all three ingredients were important and that without coaching, the vision was at risk.

On Friday morning, three weeks after the awards ceremony, Rhonda received a call from Miss Scallpell. The call was received with pleasure. Miss Scallpell had become a friend and mentor and Rhonda had no doubt it would be a sad day when she retired. *What a change since my first encounter with Miss Scallpell,* she thought.

"Rhonda. Would you come down to Phil's office?"

"Sure. What's happening?"

"Nothing urgent—but do come to Phil's office if you aren't busy."

"I'll be right there," said Rhonda.

"Thanks for coming down," said Phil. As soon as Rhonda set foot in his office, she was given a small stack of cards, elegantly hand-lettered.

"Chad has been working overtime with his team and

it took them a while to figure out something to do," began Phil. "Now I'll let Chad explain how he envisions us putting the cards to use."

"Here's the deal," said Chad. "When it comes to coaching there is no recognition of hierarchy or seniority. We all have the same responsibility: to coach without reference to position and to receive coaching without discrimination. We also have the right to accept or reject the coaching we receive.

"Coaching is not an ego trip but a responsibility we each have to help keep the vision strong. Coaching will keep the conversations real and help us make work a reward and not just a way to rewards.

"We are now going to the sixth floor to start a week-long coaching effort. Each of us will explain what's on the card to one other person and then give that person the whole rest of our stack of cards. They will need to do the same—but each person has to find a new person to receive their remaining stack, someone who hasn't been given a card before.

"Take a look at the cue card and see if you have any questions."

COACH IT CUE CARD

Have you enrolled in the vision of Good Samaritan and begun the search for your IT?

Are you willing to accept coaching from anyone who has an idea that might help you better live the vision?

Are you willing to coach others?

Do you acknowledge each person's right to accept or reject the coaching?

Will you ask for coaching when you need it?

Can you think of coaching examples from your work? (Make this a two-way exchange.)

Are you ready to become a part of the Coaching Crew?

Now it is your turn. Take the rest of this stack of cards and give it to one other person. Keep one card.

Be sure to share your own coaching stories with that person and ask him or her to do the same.

Good Luck!

They were off to the sixth floor. Within three days, everyone on the floor had received a card.

The End?

And the vision at Good Samaritan is still alive today. It lives one conversation, one vision moment, and one coaching session at a time. The model established on six served as a base from which the principles spread throughout the hospital and then throughout the hospital system. There is no question that initiating a significant change is difficult and satisfying. But when the change you worked so hard to achieve begins to fade, the ultimate challenge appears: sustaining that change as the gravity pull of old ways of being starts to exert itself. This is when the long-term winners claim the ultimate prize. Getting change to STICK!

FIND IT
LIVE IT
COACH IT

And enjoy the benefits of your hard work for a long time.

until we take action. We demonstrate our commitment by taking the following actions:

FIND IT LIVE IT COACH IT

DEDICATION

On November 12, 2000, I was packing my bags and about to leave for Turkey when the call came that every parent dreads. A coroner in San Bernardino asked if I had a daughter Beth, and then proceeded to tell me that Beth Ann Lundin had been killed in the early hours of the morning on a desolate stretch of highway between Las Vegas and Los Angeles. She was thirty-one years old and she was living her dream in Hollywood, where she worked as a set designer. Her life ended in the amount of time it takes a drunk driver to lose control of his car. A drunk driver who then drove away and left her to die in a ditch.

You search for something to hang on to in such times: a picture, a memory, a story. There was no shortage with

Beth. She lived life to its fullest and the stories were many. The one I have chosen to share in this dedication I heard at her memorial service, which was held on the beach at sunset in Playa del Rey, California. As we assembled with her friends to celebrate her life, a young man came up and introduced himself. He said he had only known Beth for one short production, but felt that after the five weeks he knew her better than he knew many people he had worked with for years. He said she was always talking about this strange-sounding book that her dad had written, *FISH!* When she died he bought and read *FISH!* and he wanted to tell me that Beth lived the principles of FISH! He said, "Beth *was* FISH!"

There is a hole in my heart and an empty space in my life. I often wear her birth ring when I speak and feel that her spirit is with me when I talk about her vibrant brand of life. Beth's candle burned brightly on this earth, and in the early morning hours you can still see the glow on the horizon. After all, she was FISH! I love you and miss you, Bethy. You are my teacher and my inspiration.

S. L. (Dad)

ACKNOWLEDGMENTS

This is our third book and we have learned that having a successful book is a team effort. We are humbled and gratified to have a team that has stayed together and gotten stronger. Our editor, Will Schwalbe, from Hyperion, is world class and his suggestions are always imaginative, important, and thoughtful. The team at Hyperion includes Bob Miller, Ellen Archer, Jane Comins, Michael Burkin, Kiera Hepford, Mark Chait, Sharon Kitter, and David Lott. And we also need to thank the awesome AOL Time Warner Book Group Sales Force.

Our agent, Margret McBride, is also our biggest fan and we love her for her intellect, her energy, and her enthusiasm. The team at McBride includes Donna DeGutis, Renee Vincent, and Faye Atchinson.

We would also like to thank the large, talented, and growing ChartHouse Learning team—especially Patrick North, for his great design, and Phil Strand and Betsy Perkins, for their terrific suggestions.

David Whyte continues to live in my head and guide much of what I write with his gentle Irish lilt. He graciously allowed us to include his poem "The Journey."

The three of us are blessed to have spouses who understand and even enjoy the ups and downs of artistic endeavor. Thank you, Gaye Christensen, Mary Paul, and Janell Lundin, for your love and support. It is so deeply appreciated.

Bring the FISH! Philosophy
deeper into your organization

ChartHouse Learning has created a family of amazing resources to help you bring the many benefits of the FISH! Philosophy into your life at work. These resources include the award-winning films FISH!, FISH! STICKS, and FISH! TALES as well as books, live learning presentations and FISHin' Gear. To learn more, visit us at:

www.fishphilosophy.com

Have you been inspired by the FISH! Philosophy at work, school or home? Are you doing anything differently because of the FISH! Philosophy? If you have a story you would like to share, contact us at:

fishtales@charthouse.com

At ChartHouse Learning, our goal is to inspire people to an awareness that transforms their experience of work and life into one of deep aliveness and purpose. For more about ChartHouse learning programs, visit:

www.charthouse.com

CHARTHOUSE
LEARNING

1-800-328-3789

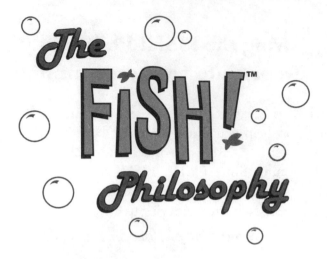

Looking for a speaker?

Are you interested in having one of the authors speak to
your organization or group about the FISH! Philosophy?
Here's how to find out about our availability
or to contact us:

Steve Lundin:
steve@charthouse.com

John Christensen:
john@charthouse.com

Harry Paul:
thepauls@cox.net

or **speakers@charthouse.com**

Over 2 million combined copies in print and still swimming!

The original book that made a huge splash around the world tells the story of a fictional company that transformed itself by applying lessons learned from Seattle's famous Pike Place Fish market.

THE WALL STREET JOURNAL BUSINESS BESTSELLER

Catch the Energy & Release the Potential

FiSH!

A Remarkable Way to Boost Morale and Improve Results

Work Made F... Gets Done

Stephen C. Lundin, Ph.D.,
H... Paul, and John Christensen
...

0-7868-6602-0

≋ FiSH! TALES ≋

The ofFISH!ial follow-up to the runaway national best-seller Fish! offers exciting, dramatic, real-life stories of how companies and individuals apply the "Fish! Philosophy" to boost morale and improve the quality of their businesses and lives.

Real-Life Stories to Help You Transform
Your Workplace and Your Life

FiSH! TALES

The #1 Way to Boost Morale

Bite-sized stories,
Unlimited possibilities.

Stephen C. Lundin, Ph.D.,
John Christensen, and Harry Paul,
bestselling authors of FISH!
with Philip Strand

0-7868-6868-6

At bookstores now
⊞ HYPERION   FishPhilosophy.com

The FiSH! Philosophy:

Play ✖ **Make Their Day** ✖ **Be There** ✖ **Choose Your Attitude**

NOTES